THE MAGNIFICENT VANISHING ACT

Matt Riker grew up in Switzerland, Sweden and England. He started writing poetry while studying English and History at the University of Berne in Switzerland. Matt has lived in Bangkok, Cape Town and in and around Berne, where he currently works as a teacher and university lecturer. A polyglot and keen traveller, he also passionately believes in balancing body and mind through martial arts, enjoys surfing and has a keen interest in intellectual pursuits of different kinds, including languages, philosophy, history, culture and art. This is his first collection.

The Magnificent Vanishing Act

Matt Riker

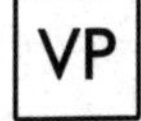

Valley Press

First published in 2023 by Valley Press
Woodend, The Crescent, Scarborough, YO11 2PW
www.valleypressuk.com

ISBN 978-1-915606-11-2
Cat. no. VP0211

A CIP record for this book is available from the British Library.

Cover and text design by Peter Barnfather.
Cover artwork: *The Blue Rigi, Sunrise*, 1842,
Joseph Mallord William Turner 1775–1851. Photo: Tate.

Printed and bound in Great Britain by
Imprint Digital, Upton Pyne, Exeter

for Katja

Contents

Acknowledgements

Among all those who have contributed to this book in some way, I wish to explicitly thank:

Katja, for her love, her interest and support.

Eva, Karin, Kim, Simon and Stephan, for making poetry happen.

Richard Begbie and Elsa Fischer, friends and fellow poets, with whom I have worked over the last few years. Without their feedback, both honest and sharp, personal and empathetic, I would not have come this far, in every way. Read their poems.

I.

prologue

Starfish

i.

At low tide on an afternoon
we walked along the beach
and found a colony of starfish
half-hidden in the sand.

We picked up one of them, then more
and let them crawl across
our hands and arms. We marvelled
at their alien symmetry,
the toughness of their mottled skin.

No brain to steer them—still
their many feet marched on
in aimless unison, eager little soldiers
in translucent white battalions.

ii.

That very hour you lay
thousands of miles away, supine
on the table in the theatre, dead still,
the baroque chambers of your skull
exposed as latexed hands
gripped razor blades and cut.

iii.

I walk into your ward. Travel
back in time. Inside me there's
a catalogue of moments. I feel
I have forgotten something
that I maybe never knew. I'll try
to talk, divert you for some time.

At your door I take a breath
to brace myself but pause.
My hand resting
on the clean steel handle
feels detached.

iv.

A boxer's helmet covers
your trepanned skull.
One arm hangs limp
like the lost limb of a starfish
on that beach. The strip light
makes you look so pale it seems
that I could look right through.
Your skin's thin veil is holding you

together. One side of you refuses
all commands. You lie askew
as I embrace you awkwardly.

v.

We most resemble ships.
There is a wind that moves us
but resists prediction. The sea
is full of wonders but will not be
tamed. The ships seem strong,
but look how many wrecks.

II.

and into that flickering life that is his

Moths Drink the Tears of Sleeping Birds

from an article in the New Scientist

Soundless he flits past the trunks of the trees
in this night of the forest.

In the distance—asleep on a branch—
is a bird that he senses, then sees and approaches:

it is a she-bird, huge, even now her feathers
spectral, iridescent, metal-tinged.

He alights at the eye near the corner,
the mouth of that channel of dreams

and where they condense to nacreous tears,
to shimmering mother-of-pearl.

He drinks of these tears and he enters
her dream and her body is his.

Still unsure of his strength, of the lift of her dream,
he flaps a few times, like she did when young

and leaving her nest. Then steadily beating her wings
he flies up and breaks through the ceiling of leaves

into the sky where he glides without fear.
The moon high above is his compass,

his guide. He sails out the night
till the wash of the morning passes the rim

and then he descends in a tightening spiral,
passing the treetops into the forest

down to the branch where she sleeps,
and before she awakes

he slips out of her dream
and into that flickering life that is his.

Still drunk on the dream he takes off, flits away
and hides in a crevice in the trunk of a tree

as old as the day that has broken again.
And he waits for the night.

Clearing

This is where we live
the forest of the world
where we begin in darkness
covered tight
and then first light
but still there is a canopy above
that keeps us safe

Later as the branches part
we see a patch of blue expand
and as the sunlight reaches us
we grow and swell

And as we start to move
the trees move out
a glade appears
and we get space and time

Change: there is more light
more air
but nothing to protect us
from the sky

In praise of trees

For once I will not praise the animal
but I will praise trees: the feel

of their bark, how they rise
far above us mapping the past,

each trunk its own story. How storied
they stand. How they seem

always unmoved and rooted in time,
not as we are—restless and thin.

How they doggedly grow, clutching
the rock, how their grip doesn't slacken.

And still we disdain their static
existence. Their lack of a brain. Yet look

how they learn—memories caught in the core
of their cells. Those polymer cells, how

they make their own food. And their different
speed, the size of their breath. How

they speak to each other in their chemical
language, plumbing their world.

Keeping time

The clock that keeps the time for us
is broken. The world flattens
as it exponentially accelerates.

But listen for the prosody
of all things living: the impatient
wriggle of tadpoles in a pond,
the swallow's swooping arc,
the helicopter seeds of sycamores,
the sloe's black thorns that punctuate
its glut of flowers. The scent

of honeysuckle mesmerises
me. Looking more closely, I find
syncopation in each moment.

Southern gastric-brooding frog

There was a frog in Australia
that did no harm, no good.
When it disappeared
no one really missed it.
This frog would keep its froglings
in its stomach. No other animal does this.
Strange and quirky, the idea appeals.

The world is always ending
somewhere. Beginning somewhere else.
When things outlive their moment they will go.

Outside my window the morning is autumnal,
the world a little blander.

Tokyo Express

*In 1997, the Tokyo Express was hit by a rogue wave
en route from Rotterdam to New York and lost cargo,
including almost five million Lego pieces.*

There's a dragon on the beach.
No need for panic. Lego flotsam—
it's small and green and made
of brittle plastic. I take it
between my index finger
and my thumb. A little bleached,
a little worn by sand and salt.

The stories it could tell
of things adrift
in the currents down below.

I'm sure it bears a message
the colour of corals
and anemones, thick like
oarweed, tangle kelp,
telling of jellyfish spawning,
the seal's return to the sea,
the eel's perennial journey,
the lobster and the crab.

I clench my fist
around the dragon,
pocket it. Walking home,
I feel it chafe
against my skin.

Eocene

There is a web that slants
into the widening world
between unrolling leaves of fern.
A spider lies in ambush
till an awkward fly is snagged.
Clicking into action,

the spider moves
to kill. And then
from somewhere in the trees
a drop of resin drips and captures
both in amber, coincident,
forever in the still life of their death.

Swordfish

They heaved a giant swordfish in,
laid it heavy on a wooden table.
The smooth skin of the fish was flawless,
its huge eyes broken but unclouded.
Were they a mirror or a well?

I saw a blue that had no closeness
and no distance—a hostile, shimmering space.
The creatures there were utterly unlike us:
freed from gravity, unaffected by the layering
of rock and earth and air. Grown bizarre.

No falling but in death,
rising only on the evolutionary scale.
This world contained itself.
                             I moved away.
The gleaming scales were drying fast.

The Magnificent Vanishing Act

The clowns are done, the acrobats,
the aerialist hanging from
her flying trapeze, the juggler
spinning plates on sticks, swaying
on his one-wheeled bicycle,
and the contortionist, reptilian
in her twisting sequinned dress.
Rapturous applause. The director
steps forward to announce:
This will be our last act for tonight.

In a top hat and a suit of midnight
satin, his white shirt gleaming
in the light, the magician enters.
Above the sawdust of the ring,
motes swirl in the light.
Three glass bowls are carried in
and set out on a table in a row.

In the first, a pair of bright
green frogs, skin grainy,
eyes silver in the arc lamps' glare,
the black slit of their pupils violent,
a gash. With a flourish of the orchestra,
the great magician flings a cloak
over the bowl, removes it
and the frogs are gone.

In the next bowl, water magnifies
the plated body of a fish,
firm and muscular and tight.
The floodlight glances off its scales.
Fins balancing, it remains suspended
until the cloak descends again.
And then it vanishes.

In the last bowl there's a bird,
beaked with ivory, its feathers
red-tipped, blue-black, metallic,
its dark claws clicking on the glass.
It croaks. The cloak falls
and is lifted. Nothing remains.

And then the great magician bows
and pulls the cloak across himself.
The audience holds its breath.
Losing all support, the cloak
flutters empty to the ground.

In the circus tent the lights go out.

Anthropocene

A haze in the sky.
Soot on the cars.
My woollen coat is
covered in ash. I lick
it from my sleeve.
It is dry and I choke.

What is the wind
that carried it here?
Where is the fire
that made the soot?

There will be cities
beyond the horizon, burning.
Smouldering peat.
Forests in flames.
A layer will mark us all
in time. We will remain.

What is the wind
that carried it here?
Where is the fire
that made the soot?

III.

and in our sleep the house begins to tilt

The interview

I stared at my computer. I'd swallowed
a pill to calm me. I watched
the count-up to the interview, clicked
the link and saw six faces on my screen,
some smiling, some serious, all surreal.

They asked me questions, made me talk
of how I'd do the job, of my philosophy
and dreams, the minutes ticking by, until
the wispy-haired professor caught me
entirely off guard: *Turn the screen,*
he said, *show us your desk.* I did not want
to show my desk but could not see
how to get out of this. I prevaricated,
tried evasion, offered them a view
of my neatly ordered library. Nothing
helped. And so I turned my screen
towards the piles of books, the paper
mess, the stains and empty coffee mugs.

I faced the screen again. And then
the sallow director in her yellow blouse
enquired about my legs. *Are they good legs?*
she asked. I couldn't think of what to say.
And so she told me to stand up and point
the camera down. Reluctantly I did so,
rising slowly, my white shirt barely
covering my underwear. My naked legs
were pale. *Is that enough?* I said.
Six heads nodded on my screen
and told me they'd consider
my application in the coming days.
Then six mouths thanked me
for my efforts, and six hands
waved goodbye in unison.

State of emergency

I walked last Monday through the centre
of the city. The sun stood high, the daylight
wore a wide, wild grin. But no one there

to see it. How easily our cities fall.
Each morning we assume that everything
goes on. But then a flagstone cracks

and somewhere else a wall caves in
and in the temple oak beams rot
and in our sleep the house begins to tilt.

Think of King Alaric, surrounded by his simpletons
who must have been amazed to walk in the debris
of Rome—the thoroughfares thick with blood and shit

and plunder—who must have gaped, wide-eyed,
at all those splendid monuments, at shrines
and halls and baths and offices. Just a month before
they'd seemed so solid and self-evident.

After Boccaccio

from The Decameron

The sky is clear. I see Orion rise
above my compost bin. That's how far
I go these days. I mostly stay indoors

> *Most of them remained in their houses,*
> *either through poverty or in hopes of safety,*
> *and fell sick by thousands.*

and talk to people only on a screen. I avoid
the crowds. We're told to stay at home
though deaths are not so many.

> *Since they received no care and attention,*
> *almost all of them died.*
> *Many ended their lives in the streets*

It's spring. I have an urge to climb
some mountaintop in Africa, to see
the tip of Stromboli spit fire

> *both at night and during the day;*
> *and many others who died in their houses*
> *were only known to be dead because*

or, like Boccaccio, write a book that lasts,
create a work of art, or finally read the great
philosophers. In bed I watch *A Life on Our Planet*.

> *neighbours smelled their decaying bodies.*
> *Dead bodies filled every corner.*

Traveller

I wish to know the world, and soon.
But no, we're in a lockdown now.
In satellite mode on Google Maps
I spin the globe, zoom in and out and follow
routes to places I have never been.

I peer at lonely beaches from above,
the impenetrable surface of the sea.
I think of what it's like to walk through
Bangkok, Cairo or New York
and switch to Street View and I'm almost there.
What draws me in are often names:

Ashkelon and Zanzibar
and Muscat, Cochin, Union's End,
Mount Disappointment, the Antipodes.

It's all I have right now.
They say we truly travel only
with the mind. But I just want to go.
It's getting dark outside. I get up
to pour some tea and navigate
my limited geography.
I find it stranger than before.

IV.

just this once and not again

Shore walk

My feet are cold as I try to keep my balance
on the shingle slope that tilts towards the sea.

Along the beach wild geese take off
in their oracular formation. There's flotsam scattered
everywhere. I feel the tide inside me rising up
and falling. I want to clutch at the horizon
but the seascape changes every second
as it moves towards me like a continent.

The shingles hiss. The birds, the surf,
all static. In the backlight of the morning,
salt spray turns to mist.

Night at the beach

And then I walked away from you
down to the water. Underneath my feet
the shingle's crunch, ahead of me the sea.
The waves were hissing in the dark. I could only
see their whitened crests, could only hear their crash.
I felt a sense of longing and of loss—though what it was
I'd lose or lost I couldn't say. I envied those who'd come to rest,
or who moved forever sideways, like the crabs. In the distance
there was light: oil rigs, wind farms, fishing boats. I wanted
to escape and closed my eyes and there I was: Around
me wind was howling, the turbine's giant blades
were spinning fast. I turned around and saw,
it seemed, a thousand spinning turbines,
turning, whirring till I could no longer
see or listen and it all went dark.

Flight

that dream
again

of almost flying

of standing on the ledge
and letting go
and falling

falling
until you almost hit the ground
and then you feel
know

that it would take
just one flap of your wings
and you could fly

but then
you wake

Voracity

That things should not be blurred or dull,
but sharp. I remember a city
in the tightest knot of night, before
the dark begins to rupture.

We were all drunk on music and on sleeplessness
and it was closing time and suddenly we ran,
raced, first through streets, then narrow lanes,
then trees, up to the castle on the hill above.
High on the ruins of the curtain wall we perched,
looking down. The city quiet beneath us,
nothing moving in the streetlights' orange glow.

We sat there wide awake with daring,
with giddiness, with joy, with company,
with the ease and clarity of everything,
right then.

Commerce

I was walking in loops through
streets where paint flaked off
the walls and buildings crumbled
with the rot of long monsoons.
I entered a bazaar,

a shapeless parcel in my hands,
battered and wrapped in dirty cloth.
On it I read *Love* in many languages,
carefully crossed out each time.
A ragged man came up to me,
mouth betel-stained, his teeth
all gone. He asked me:

Is it for sale? Some people
might pay well. No haggling
though, not even over love.
He turned and vanished.

I stood there, parcel heavy
in my hands, could not decide.
I felt the dread of losing things.

Human

I walk along a street still black and wet
with rain. In front of me a slug
slogs its way across a tarmac plain.

Some days I want to dangle puppies
by their tails and watch them try
to wriggle free. On other days,
I feel like strangling kittens
or squeezing lab mice till they squeak.

I am human. That makes me
what I am, not who I want to be.
We grow around our conscience
till we are respectable and civilised,
but in our marrow we're still animal.
We eat the heart of things.

It's time to whet the knives,
to let the bellows blow. It's Sunday
and the roast will soon be served.
I want to eat it rare and red and juicy.

The slug hasn't moved much farther.
I take a step and hover. I'll end it. Here.

Medical

A torso and four healthy limbs, lean and deft.
A cunning brain. An open mind. A heart
that knows the stakes, forever pushing on.
Clear eyes, intact or almost. Healthy skin
that tans so willingly. And underneath, the organs,
seamless in their work. Digestion normal,
not easily disrupted. Capable of reproduction if
desired. In all: sturdy, good and permanent. And yet

just one unlucky toss, one clot of blood, one cell,
one blink, one blind spot on the eye, one breath,
one swim, one drink, one thought too far, one thought
not far enough, once doesn't count (it counts),
or doesn't hurt, it's just a scratch,
a one night stand, a cigarette,
just this once and not again—
is all it takes.

I walk along the river bank.
It's early summer, there's a man
ahead of me. Thick hair, young and tall.
Passing him I see his withered arm,
useless at his side.

Escape velocity

I walk along the edge
of the escarpment
looking down. Far below,
verdant fields stretch out.
My wings of wax
are ready. They smell
of wind and leather.
I flex them. Will they hold?
It takes great cruelty to fly.

Last night all my little lies came back

to me, marching in lockstep, an unarmed phalanx
closing in. At the front, grim and silent, the ones
that I remembered, and behind them, faceless,
row on never ending row, the ones forgotten.
They were about to reach me. I became afraid
and fled. They marched on. And as I ran and ran,
I wondered where my great lies lay, and woke.

After the tally

I have remembrances of yours,
That I have longed long to re-deliver.
– Hamlet, III.1.93–94

i.

You're at the bar, locked
in conversation with a man. I
remember your face, remember
the music. The lyrics are blurred.

ii.

The pulse of a strobe
falls on the dancers
held in a frame by a trick
of the light. I want
to give in to the rhythm,
the numbness of drink.

iii.

Under the stars, the nights
expand into years. Still
I remember, there in the starlight
the warmth of your touch,
the scent of your body, its texture
and shape, a word at the right time,
the right time itself.
The sound of the snowflakes
falling, your breath
in the chill of the night.

V.

listening for the key turning

Meditation

I am small
this is my comfort:

in the turning of the wheel
that drives the millstone of the world

I am a mote of dust
that may be ground to smaller fractions

but with a thousand million other particles
will slowly make the grinding slower

and at the very end of things
will make the whole machinery

ratchet to a standstill
with a hellish noise and stop

this is my comfort:
I am small

Material

we cultivate
our own mythologies
made of bright materials

complex carbons
shiny
and sleek

they lack
metal's deep simplicity
and strength

they lack
the storied texture
that is wood

In April

The heavy snow
is not here to stay
but to remind us
that summer is mortal
and brief

and that deep underneath it
a panther is waiting
pale

for the day
when different stars
will light
a familiar dark

when it will strike
again

The pitch drop watcher

In a Brisbane lab in 1927, Thomas Parnell
set up the world's longest-running experiment.

He fills a funnel with hot pitch,
allows the bubbling bitumen
to cool and settle. Three years pass,
the funnel is unsealed and the race

begins. He waits and watches—
the funnel's mouth turns
black as pitch accretes into a drop.
Some days he thinks he sees
that drop of pitch distending
and excitement swells.
Nothing happens. Years go by.

The professor's hair recedes.
Germany, Japan advance.
The drop of pitch moves closer
to its falling till it hangs
on the funnel by a whisker.
Often Parnell watches, waiting
for his precarious drop
to fall. One night it does

and he's not there. He is asleep
in his recurring dream
where he records
the pitch drop fall.

Next day he sees it, lustrous
in its bowl of glass. He hides
his disappointment, turns
the radio on. The news
is bad yet far away.

A Global History of Aerial Bombing

I decided that today I would try to drop bombs from the aeroplane.
No one had ever tried such a thing, and if I succeed
I shall be happy to have been the first.
– Lieutenant Giulio Gavotti, Tripoli, 1st November 1911

Scouting the bookshop for an easy read
I see *A Global History of Aerial Bombing*,
on its cover the outline of a bomb. I reach for it,
separate its first few pages, read. Oh Giulio Gavotti,
now surely in the seventh circle with famous men
of war and violence, what were you thinking,
your left hand on the steering wheel, in your right
a pound of dark grey steel? As with your teeth
you pulled the safety tag and threw? As you saw
the small cloud rise from the middle of the camp?
Knowing what you did, not knowing where the race
would lead. My sons are round the corner, waiting.
I stand there, book in hand, unable to decide.

Salt

My leather shoes are stained from walking
in the slush and I'm annoyed
for they were new. *It's the salt,*
you say and make me travel back in time.

Here's bread and salt for welcome,
here's an empire to build on it, here's
your salary, legionnaire. No more. Now
it's scattered on the ground to keep
the frost away. I curse the winter
and the rain, as if it helped.

Months later in an olive grove
that overlooks Lucija saltern in the heat.
The salt pans teem with audible life:
the cry of birds, the hum and crackle
of invertebrates, the wind that stirs the reeds.

The sun sets on the saltern. Pelicans ascend,
wings singing, white as the glittering
mounds of salt. My water bottle reads:
Ideally suited for a low sodium diet.

Hunger

Looking at Apollo's torso
broken but alive, Rilke feels
that something's there.
That is what hunger is.

And this is hunger: my son
crying his lungs out for the night feed,
the world insulting him.

And that this morning at the station
a suspicion sent me looking
in the crowd.

And that I gave in to desire
even though I knew that nothing
good could come from it
was hunger too.

As when the suckling pig
is turning on the spit and
the aroma makes
our mouths run with saliva.

And the time they kept from me
the one piece of the puzzle that I needed
to figure things out for myself.
Was that hunger too?

I lie in bed, waiting
for you to arrive.
And nurse my hunger,
listening for the key
turning in the lock.

On certain days

there is inside my house a flight
of rooms removed by half
an inch in a direction
that I can't quite name
off a little at an angle,
like in the drawing of a child.
How to get there seems
impossible to figure out.
I sometimes feel the walls
and listen. I wonder if
there's something hidden
in those rooms. A corner
where the puppeteers are,
waiting for the show to start.

One minute silence

on Remembrance Day

And then everyone fell silent.
Some were sitting and some
standing, the speakers hummed
and crackled faintly and even that
at some point stopped. I thought

if only every day could end like this:
one minute silence at the hinge of midnight

and then everything still. Now might we hear the rush
of blood, its flooding through the valves, the drumbeat
of our heart. And if we listened further, closer, we'd hear
the bubbling in the bellows of our lungs, the neurons'
snap, the hiss at the synaptic gap. That, in time,

might root us, align us with the earth
and with the slow drift of the continents.

We'd hear them heave and grate below,
beyond our understanding always.
We'd hear the rainfall in the distance,
mountains letting go, rubble
being ground to silt.

Finally we'd find
our place.

VI.

the words above their graves

Horse Engraving on Bone

Exhibit in the British Museum, ca. 12,500 years old.
The only piece of Upper Palaeolithic art known
from Britain depicting an animal.

On the other side just bones:
a horse's head, scratched
onto a rib. Still, it takes me in.

My forehead almost on the glass,
I peer at it and trace the lines
until they throb with meaning and I drift.

We are the ones who carved this bone,
children in an adult world.
Night-blind with moonblink

we huddled in caves. Naked and soft
we found sleep in the safety of numbers.
In circling the fire. We closed our ranks

against the dark outside, where every
creature, every stone was joined
in hostile conference against us.

We made this world our habitat.
We named it, reined it in and broke it
into stories on the walls.

In the flickering light we sang
ourselves onto that horse, to rule
through image, word. *Mimesis*.

Our first steps into magic,
our first attempt at art.

Head music

There's music in my head, it's always there
in verses full of rhythm, wild with din.
My song resists. Metre will not tame it.
It will not be dressed up and then paraded
in the streets in chains, defanged and harmless
like a dancing bear. And it will not
be caged, forever pacing like the leopard
I once saw in Saigon zoo and pitied. No.
But outside autumn rain and summer
gone, the clouds are deep and set for writing
and everything seems possible, even
a sonnet. Here it is. Tomorrow, I'll listen
as the words fall into place again. And
in their organic order write them down.

The Grammont in the Morning Sun

Ferdinand Hodler, 1917

at the centre the mountain
in all its triangular weight
is warmed by the morning
to yellow to green

in gulleys in ravines
night persists
the dense blue chill
that in the turning of the world
is where everything is molded
where everything dissolves

But the eulogists

Tommy George, last speaker of the Kuku Thaypan
language of Australia, died in July 2016.

Most words had gone already, quietly departed
from a lack of use. For there was no one else
to talk with and here was another tongue
to speak in, a different voice inside his head.
Its words a closer fit for all the things
surrounding him now. So it was time, I think.

At festivals, thousands listened
to him, and others like him. He gave them
words they didn't get. A star,
they loved him as *a living relic*,
a linguistic treasure, loved the contrast,
white beard and wrinkled face.
But the eulogists were wrong.

Consider the Etruscans,
their statuary smiles—still, like
the words above their graves.

Dead language

futurus: paper thin
the clouds roll back

and look the sky
unfolds a distant screen

measured on a scale of blue
against the naked canvas

we find a flight of birds
and read in it a story

somewhere a roll of dice
determines something

harvest fires
on a field of stubble

one spark might set
our villages alight

On reading

Reluctantly I turn
the last few pages
of the novel, read

to the end, and pause.
I'm done. I leave the world
I've lived in for a week

or more. A home away
from home, it seemed
a better place than this.

More wondrous, filled
with possibility. If
I could, I'd swap—

would gladly move
my life between
two covers. Put it

on a shelf. And then
I'd walk into the street,
full of myself and tall

and brave and never
at a loss for words.
And passing me

a crowd of strangers,
their tales all waiting
to be told.

        I close the
book, bury it beneath
my pillow and switch off

the light. That dreams
may come, at least.

Trawling

The silt of everyday matter
clogs the canals; the inlet is blocked

by a wreck left behind by the tide
of events. You are waiting

for rain or the waves or even a flood
to clear things away. You are wrong.

It is you who must move.
Leave port. Leave all its cold

machinery behind. Sail out of sight
of the land. Cut the engines and drift.

Unreel your dragnet, trawl it
through a sea of words:

ghost sharks, fangteeth, dragonfish,
and all the nameless creatures of the deep.

VII.

taxonomies for pain

The dance

We measured steps to music
timed them to the songs

that played and played in harmony.
It was our private pulse until

a rival melody crept in,
another song, dissonance.

It was just audible, not more. I started
to suspect, looked at you

and saw a frown pass through your face
but *nothing* when I asked.

I'd heard but did not listen.
Would the band play louder, louder

as the tunes broke down
to noise, or would—to stay

untainted—one tune grow
softer, yield, and stop?

No. Our steps began to falter
but soon picked up again. Then

a mad and savage dance we trod
a dance beyond all tunes,

beyond all music. Eardrums burst. Blood
began to trickle down our necks.

Frenzy

Whilst I, my sovereign, watch the clock for you.
   – William Shakespeare, Sonnet 57

Each place its own inventory of loss.
In the crowd I glimpse your face
and look again—there is a stranger

wearing it. In the chatter of cafés
I hear your voice, in the whine of air vents
and the humming of the wires.

Rush hour at the station and I'm startled
by your perfume. In vain I search
for you among the passengers.

Your breath is in my bloodstream.
It hovers on my lips. I see you
half reflected in a window.

*

After we parted, your scent
still lived a while on my skin.
Impermanent tattoo of frankincense.

Happy he who forgets. I create
failed distractions, taxonomies
for pain. It's time—I close my eyes

and on the inside of my eyelids
I slowly let your face dissolve.

On Holkham Beach

We walked along the beach for miles.
The tide was out and we went barefoot
in the sand, still innocent though in suspense.
Feeling cold, we stopped behind a dune for shelter.

On the sloping sand, body next to body,
our skin soaked up the spare warmth of the sun
in temporary refuge. We knew the wind
would turn, forcing us to relocate.
Birds of passage moving south.

Last night

Because I am awake before you
I see you sleep beneath the surface
of the water. On sudden wings
I circle over you until I fold up tight,
dive and break the water—
and catch you, glittering, writhing.

For a moment we struggle
till limp with exhaustion
you slip from my grasp
and escape past the waves
back into sleep.

       My feathers
feel the wind. It's getting up
and veering. A storm is out there,
closing in. It will batter us,
but not together. I'll stretch
my wings and hover,

not knowing how to land.

Terra nullius

You're still asleep—I lie between
two states. Crossing the border,
I reach and with my fingertips
trace your birthmark, there
between your shoulder blades.
I map the atlas of your back.

You stir a little. I'm adrift
on your skin, thinking of how
we ended up here. One last night
together, no guide light but grief.
Astrolabes broken, we failed
at our triangulation.

Not long now and we'll rise, dress
and leave this room and in the hotel doorway
kiss abruptly. And walk away from here,
secretive, in separate directions,

taking doubtful solace in our maps
that show imagined countries,
no man's land.

Triptych of desire

i.

Your messages are on my screen
but you're a world away.
I read them hungrily, pinned
to insomnia like a butterfly.

My wings still wear invisible tattoos:
the pattern of your kisses, the brush
of fingertips, your breath, your foreign tongue.

The tattoos swirl and change from day to day
as if they were alive, they prick my skin
as if the needles were still stitching.
I wake instead of sleeping,
dream instead of waking.

ii.

Above the beach the jungle creeps
forever up the slopes, its darkness blacker
than the sky and full of noise. Brief rain
has raised a scent of rotting,
of growth. The birds have fallen
silent. I turn nightwards, out to sea.
The lights of fishing boats stake out
the invisible horizon. On the beach
crabs flit in and out of safety
in their burrows. I feel with them,
their restless scavenging, but wonder
at the radial patterns they create
in sand, signs I can't decipher.
I try to find distraction in
the here and now: the waves,
the light breeze on my skin,
the stray dogs barking.
But all the time my gaze keeps
turning to the fishing boats
and then beyond, to you.

iii.

I leave you with a kiss that says goodbye.
You briefly wake and kiss me too.
Your body's full of sleep, your hair a net
that holds me back. I have to go. Faster
than I need I take the elevator down
and walk out of the building. It is dark.

And it all comes back to me. How we took flight
in a tall and giddy tower in the middle of a city
heavy with light. That sudden rush. How we were
fluttering and quick, and moved so fast
our shadows could not catch us. How somehow still
they found us, as they always do, and how
we stumbled on them suddenly and fell.

Animals at night

At the edges of sleep we make love,
dividing up the fractions of the night.
Your sweat tastes of the sea. Half inside
a dream, half there within the world,
you're slick, our bodies yield.
Our shark teeth hooked
into each other we draw blood,
fins turning in a frenzied circle
round and round, there's something
that we want but it's impossible
to reach even though we bite
and snap. Nocturnal
animals for now, furtively
we steal each other's attributes,
the things we own.

The door, aslant

allows me to look in. Half uncovered,
you lie, a nude reclining

painted by Degas: languid
on her bed, a rucked up blanket
between her legs. I wonder—
are you naked, too, beneath your blanket?
You're deep in sleep. I can't stop looking.

You stir a little, dreaming. I hold my breath
and clench my fists. I want to be inside
your dream. Perhaps there's something there
I haven't seen, the shadow
of a former lover I might catch.
I stand there watching

                    turn away
not wanting to wake you,
jealousy rasping and raw in my guts.

VIII.

no story here

Dionysus

It's the drink you want and
can't resist; the woman's hand
that touches you. The other's eyes
that yours meet, fleetingly among the crowd,
and full of possibility; the sirens' pull,
their singing irresistible and strange. It's
moonlight on the tide, aswarm with
crabs. The crickets' rasping song.
The lion's kill. The salmon's spawn.
The war for Troy. The sack of Carthage,
Corinth, Rome. It's dried blood
on the sidewalk; last night's
vomit. The headlines
in the paper. Carnage
in the streets. Alone,
the voice of one man
falling, crying out.

Cassandra

years before it happens
and she knows
she needs no window to look out
she sees the sea on the horizon
curdle with their ships

days before it happens
and she knows
she sees herself
raped at the altar
dragged through the rubble
taken as loot

on the edge of the bed
she sits and bends
her head a little
eyes closed
against the overlap
and then draws out

first one pin
and then another
one by one until
finally her hair falls
free in mourning
for she knows

On war

Theseus has lost his thread
it caught fire turned to ash
between one turning and another

the sun has set and dusk
grows denser as he stumbles
through the half-light of the maze

towards the heart the centre
with the Minotaur
he has to slay

instinct chance or intellect
at every corner every fork
he hesitates

left or right towards away
there is no progress here to measure
lost in this labyrinth on Crete

Sirens

Salt crystallises on my belly
as it dries. My skin
prickles in the morning sun.
It's humid, hot already. I drift

and there are voices in the water
beckoning to take me where
there is no noise and death
is silent as it comes
to carry everything away.

The sirens lured Odysseus
above the water line.
But had he not been tied so tightly
to the mast he would have given in
and drowned and the story
would have ended.

I'm tied to nothing,
and the voices only speak
inside my head.
There is no story here
not even trivial danger.
What boredom does to you.
And so I let my body
quicken and I wait.

IX.

a trivial transgression

Transhumance

The deckchairs slowly fill—it's spring.
The walls are freshly whitened,
the plastic litter washed up
on the beach by winter storms
is cleared and flung behind the bend.

There is the hum of an event
about to happen. Snow is melting
on the mountains, almost like
it used to. The cattle
giving birth. The expectancy
of moving on. Early seeds
sprouting in the fields.

Cape Tripiti, Gavdos

Southernmost point of Europe

walk to the end of the world the continent's edge we arrive after hours and hours a boat on the beach a rotting hulk a wreck with writing round it that we can't decipher we board tread carefully across the treacherous planks the remains of the journey a rusty frying pan a pair of trainers bleached tangled rags we look below deck seeking a story but cannot enter there so we withdraw and on the simple beach we swim

Jetlagged in the waiting lounge

He was wearing good socks, colourful
and with a dragon labelled in Chinese.
Some businessman from Thailand, he waits
in the concourse of Qatar airport
for his flight to London. Where
the socks came from, workers operate
rattling big machines. Nightshift
has come. A woman in bright blue overalls,
rubber sandals and an orange shower cap
walks past the looms and checks
the shuttles' weaving. And from a distance,
jetlagged, I look on, about to fly
in the opposite direction. I'm wearing
plain socks made in China
or maybe Bangladesh.

Late morning in Bangkok

I walk past shacks of wooden boards,
plastic sheets, corrugated iron,
careful not to step into a puddle
or to slip. There's something cooking
somewhere on a stove. Its sweet, hot scent
is inescapable. Someone laughs. A mangy cat
is sitting on a plank, its mirror image
distorted in the oily water. In the shaded,
narrow lane, dirty children are playing
with a dog that probably has rabies
or at least that's what I'm afraid of,
unlike them.

Saturday night in Bangkok

In this sober burger joint
I'm the only customer, sitting
at the window with my
Chilli Double Western Bacon,
Medium French Fries
and imitation coke.

From the neon-heated street
a girl beckons me to come away
with her. The street is full of sleazy bars.
That must be where she wants to take me.
Something about it makes me sad.
I am not in the mood to entertain her
even with my gaze. So I look

away, down at the scattering
in front of me. The fries are
good and crispy. The meat is
juicy, if a little raw,
a trivial transgression.

I glance at where she stood
before. All I see is my reflection
in the window, the darkness
and the brightly coloured lights.

Above and below

Bored and sick of travelling. Above
the blue too uniform, below just clouds.
I doze and wake, leaf through

the inflight magazine: *Belgrade's
Rough Charm*. I turn the page and see

myself! I'm in that magazine, a photo of me,
sitting in the foreground on a bench.
Kalemegdan Park, the caption says.

I'm perplexed. I've never been to Belgrade
or to Serbia, not even close. It can't be me.

I stare at the figure in the photograph. I know
myself: countless mornings in the mirror, pictures
from any place but Serbia. It can't be me.

It is. I try to make some sense of it
in vain. We land, I take the magazine with me.
I'll delve into this. Research, explore.

But for some reason once at home I'm restless
and uneasy, slip into distraction. The magazine
is somewhere in a drawer. I forget.

In flight

On a sky that is falling to blue the full
moon rises on an ocean of pale cloud.
It's the colour of weathered bone.
Moonlight floods the cabin
where the lights have been dimmed
for the night and the seatbelt signs
are on again for we are passing
through an area of turbulence
and I am sitting next to someone
I don't know and have no desire
to talk to because I am
thinking of you sitting
six rows behind me
also in a window seat.

On the motorway to Milan

one car in front
one on my tail
fifty miles out

clasping
the steering wheel hard
I hold my course

the squealing
windscreen wipers clear
the view for a moment only

I'm alone
but for your face
next to me for an instant

lighting up
each time headlights
hit the car

On the road

You wake in the long light of the afternoon,
rise from your threadbare motel bed
and drive again, along the night's edge.
Sleep to sleep. A faulty car clock
keeps its time. Cars speed by you

in the rain, headlights blinding.
Windscreen wipers smear the world
onto the glass. Something

hurls towards you.

Thud. The deer limps off,
leaves a line of blood.

               Frozen,
you stand beside the car and gaze.
The weather bulletin comes on.
It warns you: *icy roads.*

X.

getting closer every day

Alphabet

Beside your bowls of soup, your names lie
spelt out in capital letters, sticky
with broth. I'm about to tell you
to get on with eating when I stop.

The city of Uruk. A river
flows green along the harbour quay,
the slow boats safely moored, soon
to be unloaded. In a mud-brick warehouse
dimly lit, a merchant presses signs
into the clay that seals the cargo to be his.

Sign by sign, from that moment
things unfold and here we are.

I dip my spoon into the broth and
with my fingers pick out letters.
An alphabet of grain.
Careful not to squash them, I too
spell out my name beside the bowl.

Echo

I made this ratatouille for you
and now the way you frown—
disgusted—at your dinner plate
startles me. You remind me
of when I was a child myself,
trigger things I had forgotten.

Dinner done, I browse
old photos of myself: plotless
scraps of me in places,
made-up memories of things
that maybe never happened.
People long forgotten. Echoes
faint with distance
like the memory of a dream.

You come and ask what I
am doing. I'm lost for words.
Once I was you and you
one day may be me. You're four
and unaware of this. Holding
my thoughts tight in my chest,
I lift you up and make you smile.

Divorce

We're getting closer every day.
On the grainy desk in front of me
my divorce contract lies—
clean black print on a white sheet
its phrases careful,
its paragraphs precise: misunderstandings
are to be avoided.

How different this is
to the ambiguity of the beginnings
where things would need to be unclear
to warrant an effect: a glance, a casual remark.
I weigh the contract in my hands—
it's slight.

I read the contract word for word.
It's clear to me, although
I don't know how we'll share the kids.
I mark the place and date
and sign my name
in letters hard to read.
And leave my desk, switch off
the light and try to sleep.

Locked

into a dream: my father meets me
halfway up the stairs, arms akimbo
and I'm fifteen again and know that
something's wrong but what it is I can't
recall, and he is backlit by the window
on the first floor that I cannot reach
without passing him, which for
some reason is exactly what I fear

After showering

And then I turned to
face the mirror, saw
my father, his cheekbones,
his jaw. The fold of his ears,
the ageing skin.

I looked at the mirror
fogging over till the image left
me with a shudder.
On the bathroom's
stone-cold floor, I stood

in thought. And then I turned again
and walked to where my sons
were sleeping, peered
at their familiar faces.
I could not bear
the sight for long

and so I tried to get my consolation
from the early morning,
sunlight falling
in patterns to the floor.

Travelling pills

I was twenty-something, on a visit
to a close friend. His mother
was out. Her many pills were lying
scattered on her plate for her return.
I played around, rearranged them:
the sun, a moon. Smileys.
We laughed!

The pills have travelled quite far:
they turn up on my father's plate.
It's full of them,
their cheerful colours
trying to fool me. I turn away,

go down to the cellar
for wine. When I return
with my ballast of bottles,
dinner will be ready.

Beyond sleep

They opened the grave
of my father. Within it,
they found beside the body

artefacts that would befit
a prince's tomb: a comb
of walrus bone, a staff
of iron, dragon skin,
a mirror that was blind,
a ring of clouded amber
and a crown.

I read the runes upon
the crown, and laid
myself beside him,
and the earth was closed
above us, and I slept.

Last songs

We sat around the table in the basement
of my mother's parents' home. I'd been there
often, as a child down to the breaking

of my voice, picking berries in the garden,
climbing trees and playing hide and seek.
And I'd explore inside, would look

at old photographs of Germany, my grandma's
drawings as an architect, objects without
function, all those stories stored in corners.

There they sat now with my mother
and my father and myself—
three generations. It was dark, the room

was lit by candles and the fire in the hearth.
The room was full of things: copper kettles, knives
of reindeer horn, a wooden chest I'd never opened.

They all began to sing. The songs were old,
I knew them too but with my flawed voice
(or so I thought) I did not dare to sing.

Their singing spoke to me of grief. I knew
I would not sit and listen here again,
in this same company.

Elegy (on entering the house)

Everything seemed
as it always had seemed
till I entered

the mind that had walked
to the welcome already
retreated a step

the stillness around me
soon tempered the echo of smell
wherever I went

in the house
in the garden
memories hosted a silent reception

you were there
you were gone
had gone

near the end of the winter
up north where the nights were still whetted with cold
sharpened enough for your purpose

your plan
in the snow by the steeple
to choose your personal closure

your own way of dying
with a bottle of vodka
to ease the descent

Last call

on the shores of Mälgsjön, Sweden

The path had gone. Both
your daughters had to steady you
through the thick grass to the cabin.
It looked the same: hard wind and rain
had rasped its logs to silver. Dust
lay everywhere inside.

Each year you'd come here
as a child. Summers were so light
that you forgot how short they were.

It was autumn now, the birches turning
yellow, the rowans red with fruit.
Frost was closing in, its edge
already on the wind. You lit a fire
and the three of you played cards
and talked and sang until at last
you slept. It must have been a night
so full of dreams that you woke early,

opened the door and stood still,
listening. An arctic loon
was calling from the reed beds
of the lake. No other sound but
your own breathing. Not even the wind.
That day you left.

In the guestbook I now read
your final entry, your hand
as neat as ever, or almost: *I'm glad
to have heard for one last time
the weird call of the loon.*

Was this the call I heard this morning?
I looked it up in Rehndal's book of birds.
The flyleaf held your name.

XI.

epilogue

Refractions

Green is the scent of the newly cut lawn
where we lay. It was June and the grass
was bleeding with life. Green
were our knees and our elbows
and backs. Green were our minds.
We were sated with dawn.

Blue is the private expanse
of a dream. In this dream I unfolded
my wings in a limitless space
still unclaimed, still open and
nameless and blank. I awoke
and knew I was chained to the ground.

Red is a word that I called you
one day. It was autumn, the leaves
were aflame. As the word spread
in ripples, as it echoed and failed
the leaves started falling and falling
till the branches were bare.

Yellow is the light that flooded
the room. The sun in the morning
one winter. The window was open,
the wind blowing in.
You lay there beside me
wrapped in a blanket of frost.

Violet is a memory. An evening alone
on the road in a forest. Miles until
sleep. You were there without warning,
mute in the glow of the dashboard.

I try to hold the image, but always
you elude me, slip back into the dark.

Poems previously published

The current versions of the poems listed below often differ, sometimes substantially, from the versions previously published.

'Elegy (on entering the house)' and 'Meditation' published in: Fortune-Wood, Rowan (ed.): *The Visitors & other short stories & poems*. Cinnamon Press, Blaenau Ffestiniog, 2010.

'Last Call' published in: *Oxford Poetry*, XVI.i, Winter 2015–2016

'Frenzy' published in: Eastman, Helen (ed.): 154. *154 Poems by 154 Contemporary Poets in Response to Shakespeare's 154 Sonnets*. Live Canon, London, 2016

'Refractions' published in: *Acumen*, #90, January 2018

'Commerce', 'Night at the beach', 'On the road' and 'Human' published in *Neon*, #45, May 2018

'Starfish' published in *Live Canon 2019 Anthology*, 2019

'State of Emergency' published in *Poetry Birmingham Literary Journal*, Issue 4, May 2020

'Last night all my little lies came back', 'On certain days', 'Shore walk' and 'The dance' published in *Neon*, #50, June 2020